A BONU

by the same author

BY GRAND CENTRAL STATION I SAT DOWN AND WEPT

A BONUS

Elizabeth
Smart

Elizabeth Smart

POLYTANTRIC PRESS
21 FORMOSA STREET
LONDON W9

First published in 1977 by Polytantric Press, London W9
2nd edition March 1977

Distributed by Jonathan Cape, Ltd
30 Bedford Square, London WC1

ISBN 0 224 01494 3

Printed in Great Britain by
Latimer Trend & Company Ltd Plymouth

CONTENTS

Introduction

After three decades of silence, Elizabeth Smart, author of
the classic *By Grand Central Station I Sat Down And Wept*,
has produced these poems. Do not be deceived by their
casual, throwaway style, their modest demeanor; these are
distillations of experience which only someone who has
suffered all and forgotten nothing could invoke. They have
the clarity of death-bed visions though perceived in the
prime of life. Even the Nature Notes, those botannical
observations at the back of this book have all the hallucinatory
freshness of the world – if you are leaving it, or if you
have just arrived.

Robert Graves tells the story of a mysterious wild horse
that can be glimpsed high in the mountains. It is white,
uncannily swift and has a long bushy tail. The horse is Art.
The tail is Fame. Most people ignominiously try to catch
the horse by the tail. The artist worth his salt jumps straight
on to the horse's back while its in motion – a near impossible
feat. Elizabeth Smart jumped on the horse's back years ago,
in the early forties to be precise. With these poems we see
that she is still riding.

Her novel was published in England in 1945. It was recognised
for what it was by only a few – notably Brigid Brophy
who wrote in her introduction to the paperback edition
printed by Panther in 1966: 'I doubt if there are more than
half a dozen masterpieces of poetic prose in the world.
One of them, I am convinced, is Elizabeth Smart's
By Grand Central Station I Sat Down And Wept . . . the
entire book is a wound, even when its rhythm expresses
the throb of pleasure, the pleasure is so ardent that it lays

waste the personality that experiences it . . . it is one of the most shelled, skinned, nerve-exposed books ever written.'

The fundamental Smart message, never far absent even in the most relaxed and conversational of these poems, is always to the point – she never forgets even in the midst of the banal, that we are 'hurtling towards eternity tongue-tied together'. The struggle is to remain perpetually open to feeling, despite the world's efforts to brutalise us. Certainly the price is too high; there seems to be no drop of joy without exceeding pain. But we have no alternative – unless we wish to be dead before we are dead.

The publication of this first edition of *A Bonus* is significant for me in more ways than one. Elizabeth Smart, who for many years has been living in a remote part of Suffolk, cultivating her garden – a miniature Sissinghurst – recently made one of her rare visits to London. She mentioned that she had been 'writing again' and the news excited me. I asked to read her new work and while doing so, Jay and Fran Landesman dropped in (Jay runs Polytantric Press, among other things). Waiting for his tea, Jay flipped open the manuscript which was lying on the table next to him and read the poem entitled 'A Bonus'.
'I'll publish it', he said. And did.

Posthumous recognition is not very satisfactory for a writer; Sylvia Plath did not receive her real accolades until after her death; Jean Rhys appeared to be condemned to the same fate until she was rediscovered in the sixties. With the publication of this small volume Elizabeth Smart will gain many new admirers. Cherish your copy, I am convinced that it is already a collector's item.

Jill Neville

A BONUS

There's Nobody Here But Us Chickens

When the elders die
Particularly rather strict ones
Like Auden,
There you suddenly are,
The unstrict inadequate
Old but not wise
Remainder,
Now foolish top dog,
Foolishly left
In the last musical chair.

The words, the works
Were always there.
But they change, or seem to,
When their makers are gone.
No nearer now
(No farther, either)
Than Byron or Blake or Thomas Traherne or Donne.

The metamorphosis starts
The chemical change
(Eliot, Dylan Thomas, Giacometti and Braque)
Cast up, cast down,
Settled, then disinterred,
Forward and back.
Reputations, by people with nothing to do,
Are footballs kicked down the years.
But the goals are never true.

That's one thing
(A slight diversion)
What I meant to say was this:
What about poor old us?
Nudging sixty or seventy or even more
Still hoping that Daddy will pick us up from the floor
And say Tut! Tut! There There
You should try to do better
Should certainly take more care.

Raise your groggy head from this rough dilemma in
Which you find yourself, though you are only feminine
And know if it's going to go on it's got to be you
(And a friend or colleague or two):
Nobody left alive can teach you or reprimand
(Drinking or winking or lending a helping hand
Is not what I mean), it's the empty air beyond
The headmaster's empty study. In fact the entire school's
Empty of masters, *you'll* have to make the rules.
Me? I'm only a learner, one of the fools,
Let me be caretaker, let the children take over.
You can't. You're alive. There isn't any cover.
Shoddy and shy and very unfit for power
They've died and made you an elder in this cold and unjust
        hour.

(Sorry, Empson and Barker and good Sir John:
I know you're there, but too young and flighty to lean upon.)

So their death isn't the sorrow I thought it would be, the
        passion and pain,
More the bewilderment of a child left out in the rain.

Doubt In A Garden

Scratch scratch
Clear a patch
Leave it a minute
The weeds are in it.

Why do this
When all that is
Is exquisite
And requisite?

Impose a pattern
On a slattern.
Make a shape.
Commit rape.

It's me O Lord
And I am bored.
I can't stand
The unplanned.

A tree falls
A tree rises
The death appals
The change surprises.

Is it right to change
Thistle for lily?
Rich and strange?
Or just silly?

Ouch! Says The Saint

Ouch! says the saint as he
Divests himself of the love
Of created objects.
Love! says the hippie
Chickadee dee dee dee!
But when he is bare
And shivering there
What then? says the hen.
How now? my brown cow.
What is this?
Says the instructress.
A cool snowlocked
Wisdom
Out of ear-shot
Scream and kiss.
Calm? Dead?
A better compost
Than most?

Bulbs, Corms, And Tubers

It's terrifying in spring
Observing
The unabashed egotistical
Ruthless energy
With which the bulbs thrust free.
It reminds me of the time during the war
When I felt the breath of a bomb just miss me
And careless and colossal
Destroy the house next door.
And though I seem much stronger than any eranthis
Or fragile daffodil, and I have felt force
Or fire or passion, perhaps something worse,
Drive me blindly on,
Yet nothing nothing at all
To compare with a cyclamen.

Plants are millions and millions of years older than us
But they never practise self-abuse.
They don't commit suicide, though they sometimes despair
And decide that the life before them is unfair
And let themselves die. And they can have moods.
But these are mostly alien plants from other latitudes,
Bewildered, and with rhythm all askew
Like aeroplane travellers losing whole days in the blue
Never to be recaptured. Plants in their native lands
Have a thousand tricks and dodges to withstand
Enemies and accidents and they have the humility
To let this earth-shaking energy pass through free;
They never tell lies or pretend
They haven't met with a setback when they have. They bend
Twist, turn, hurry on propagation,
Seeding must be seen to, they're mad about creation.

If it can't be done with happy open petals in the sun
It will be done with smaller less happy ones but it will be
    done.
They'll see to it that the bee finds them, the bug and the
    butterfly,
And then with a sigh of contentment they'll be content to
    die
And let the next rampant livers come on and perform:
Enormous grasses, thistles, even, devious bindweed. Then
    bulb and corm
Or tuber goes into a long modest unegotistical rest
Gets baked, soaked, frozen, and doesn't care in the least.
It sits quietly quietly through months in this retreat.
Then suddenly! suddenly! the message comes! Then!
Then! It can burst through concrete!

The Rhythm And The Rhyme

The rhythm and the rhyme
If the concentration is absolute
They obey the thought
With a little help afterwards.
But for wobbly concentration
The puzzle forms the strictness
Acts like iron lungs
Props to start up breathing.
One a mad pursuit.
One a sly strategy.

A Bonus

That day that I finished
A small piece
For an obscure magazine
I popped it in the box

And such a starry elation
Came over me
That I got whistled at in the street
For the first time in a long time.

I was dirty and roughly dressed
And had circles under my eyes
And far far from flirtation
But so full of completion
Of a deed duly done
An act of consummation
That the freedom and force it engendered
Shone and spun
Out of my old raincoat.

It must have looked like love
Or a fabulous free holiday
To the young men sauntering
Down Berwick Street.
I still think this is most mysterious
For while I was writing it
It was gritty it felt like self-abuse
Constipation, desperately unsocial.
But done done done
Everything in the world
Flowed back
Like a huge bonus.

Trying to Write

Why am I so frightened
To say I'm me
Any publicly acknowledge
My small mastery?
Waiting for sixty years
Till the people take out the horses
And draw me to the theatre
With triumphant voices?
I know this won't happen
Until it's too late
And the deed done (or not done)
So I prevaricate,
Egging them on and keeping
Roads open (just in case)
Go on! Go on and do it
In my place!
Giving love to get it
(The only way to behave).
But hated and naked
Could I stand up and say
Fuck off! or, Be my slave!
To be in a very unfeminine
Very unloving state
Is the desperate need
Of anyone trying to write.

Babies

Granny told me
About her nine
Children
Emotional mist in her eyes.

But if she went into Barnardos
And they were each in a cot
(By magic – they're grown-up now)
Would she know which ones she'd got?

Growing is the strange death
In life that nobody mourns
The forgotten babies that filled the whole world
When they were first born.

Inside The Bearded Man

Inside the bearded man
The crying baby lies
The disarming face is gone
The flowery flesh is worn
And nobody wants to rush in
To his peevish petulant cries
And wipe his bottom or eyes.

He's in a pitiful mess
But the middle-aged man
No matter how hard he tries
Cannot command the love
That came free with his innocence.
He bawls in vain in his pain
Such comfort will never never come again

I Want To Leave A Message

Are you there?
No, you're not in.
Then I'd like to leave a message:
For if and when we meet
I might be lighting the fires
Or cooking a mess of potage
Or making a dozen beds.
The moment is seldom right
And from action and omission
Which I thought would be full of clues
It's a lot to expect
That others would guess my news.
To me it seemed loud and clear
But it could corroborate error
To you, if you didn't choose
Decoding, wartime, terror.

In My Shattered Garden

In my shattered garden
I lie and cry.
Why?
I could scrub floors
And get a sense
Of something done
A neat
Achievement
But
I get up
And stumble on
And get slapped back.
I count my blessings
Many, many.
It is no use.
Back and forth
I pace
Carrying a deep despair
Like a fretful child.
There there, despair,
There there.

Is This Pain Justified?

Is this pain justified?
Set like a monstrous stillbirth
In a Christmas panic –
An unwrappable
Un-depth-chargable
Gloom.
If memory worked
More than a three-day week
Euphoria would step in
And be my sparkling guest
But I can't recall my loves
And all the old toast-warm
Encouragements.
Courage is the word
But it takes all I have
To carry faith
Like an undernourished twin
To overfed despair.

Only a few hours more
And people and bustle
Will dispel this state.
Flat facts. I know. But know? Truly? No.
I won't reveal this sin
Of unjustified suffering,
Four days of wallowing
In an obscene affair
With a bully who takes advantage
Of me when no-one is there.

How I used to long
For silence and solitude.
Because in a day or two
Out of the blue
Angels descended then
Connecting me with heaven
In a constant consummation,
Independent of men
And things and events
All day and night
A long long amen.

Now they've flown
As is their wont.
Why should they return?
How can I expect
Their brilliant rescue work?
I don't. I feel they've quit
And quite rightly
Why should they flirt
With a psyche so unsightly
Connecting wires pulled out
And electric knowledge gone?

Rooks reel
In a barren field
Heifers munch
Little birds crouch
In a cold bush
The clock ticks
The walls groan
Every tree
Signals futility.

Parcels Christmas-wrapped
Are full of trash.
Weak spirit and weaker flesh
From every sight
The message comes in a flash:
Despair is everywhere.

So what is this pain about?
This unjustified suffering?
Why don't I know
Why I suffer so?
Pacing pacing
The small room
Blind deaf and dumb
Warped by gloom.

Is There A Message For Me?

I wanted to leave a message
But now I say
Is there a message for me?
Please see.
Look everywhere
Scour out the cubbyholes
Scoop out the stuff at the back
Search through the notes on the desk
And papers squashed in the grass
Did no-one no-one
Leave a word for me?
Or telephone when I was out?
Or tell somebody something
To tell me when we met?
Not yet?
I can't understand.
Is the post on strike?
The telephone out of order?
I had some friends
And some of them promised to write.
I felt very pampered and rich
It was almost a surfeit.
How could I have then foreseen
This December evening
And my desperate need
For a pulley out of this pit?
If the message should come
Look for me under the ground.

There Are Two Movements In A Woman's Life

Rock rock
Rub rub
Two movements
Life's hub.
Soothe pain
With a rock.
Make clean
With a rub.
Be rubbed
For love.
Be rocked
For shock.
In a rub
The vigorous hand
From side to side
In aggressive stand.
But real aggression
Comes from above.
Vertical is pain.
Vertical is love.
But horizontal
To keep clean.
Horizontal
To lullaby.
From side to side to still the cry
To ease the ache to dull the pain
From side to side from side to side
Rocking and rubbing the women ride.

Christmas Is Coming

Under the cracked and cobwebbed walls
Into the cold and dirty rooms
To sit on torn and broken chairs
Christmas is coming.

I'll put on a black cloak covered in hairs
Joss-sticks to camouflage the fumes
And wrap up rubbishy plastic dolls
Christmas is coming.

The many things I need appals
The horror of the undone looms
I haven't even swept the stairs.
Christmas is coming.

Light fires light fires and say your prayers
That the spirit will kill these crouching glooms
And the heart be singing its madrigals.
Christmas is coming.

Cleanliness Is *Not* Next To Godliness

Godliness
And cleanliness
Were joined by the devil
To do evil.
Poverty
Can never be
Clean, nor can
Misery.
Snot and tears
Piss and shit
Usually
Accompany it.
Soap costs money
So do baths;
Are for the haves
Not the not-haves.
The minute your house
Is shining clean
Pride rises up
And comes between
You and God,
And self-esteem
Is your new
Unholy dream.
If clean is pleasant
In your eyes,
Clean, but then
Apologise.
Cleanliness, like lust
Drink, food
Is beautiful
But not of God.

Accumulation

Boredom and guilt
Drive one on
In a slow
Accumulation.

How weak are vanity
Lust and ego.
But it wasn't like this
For Victor Hugo.

Men find power
An ignition
Cast off cares
Of accumulation.

But that's for living
For getting by:
Pleasure! Nature
is trite and sly.

But seek the pearl
O oyster soul.
The whole the hole
The hole the whole.

Horror and terror
Nightly seen
But in between
Serene! Serene!

They talk right
Now of survival
But trees wait.
Join the right side.

When a word's in the air
It's indication:
Catastrophe reaching
Consummation.

The slow slow play
The turgid novel
The cautious poem
Are infidel.

And useless too
Decades late:
Nothing there
To accumulate,

Just catching a whiff
After the lion
Hunters.
Tatterdemalion!

A Terrible Whiteness

Every writer
Except flibbertigibbets
Feels the horror
Of the blank page.
Out of a million million permutations
To pull the three or four words
That move into a nucleus –
How can it be done?
Pressing down on the nerves
Like bursitis
Something wants to get out.
Lance in the wrong place
And you do not get release
But aggravation
And loss of concentration.
Envy the bold surgeon
With his sharp knife
Smiling and certain above the white body.

CPS & JBP
'A book should serve as an axe for the frozen sea within us' Kafka

No frozen seas are locked within
CPS and JBP
They write with pleasure sweet as sin
Not like me oh not like me
I'm anguished to know how to begin
Held in horror like a gin
Every word an agony
Yet not to write a treachery
What would you do JBP
If you were me if you were me?

Why is it easy, CPS?
Where is the boredom? Where the mess?
Just neat white paper covered with words
Or are they turds or are they turds?

Have you a trick to teach me, please,
About releasing the frozen seas?
Have you an axe that's sharper than mine?
Or an understanding with the divine?
A pact with the Muse? A discipline?
Or does it depend on what's within?

Within CPS and JBP
Things must be very orderly.
Everything flows and nothing baulks
They take the Muse for domestic walks
Pile up pages like games of golf
Strenuous maybe but satisfying
(Some people don't even know they're lying)
A tiny triumph every day
That is the way that is the way.

Don't go exploring don't dig deep
Eschew all friendships with the worms
Learn the ropes and nautical terms
And watch the weather for dangerous storms
Then like me you'll never be
Locked in the sea locked in the sea
CPS and JBP.

Little Magazines

Hungry red-wristed
Keepers of the true
Small unsentimental tone
Or thread or litmus paper
That in the midst of madness
Or chaos or revolution
(When passions obscure
And everyone repudiates
What he knew)
Steadily sturdily
Keep a small-sized
Truth in view
(Small-sized is
The embryo too):
Them I salute
Because we can't go out on a limb
Without guardians
Like them.
Eddie Linden, for instance,
Let us hymn.

To Patrick Kavanagh On Reading His Poem 'Is'

Paddy Kavanagh
How right you are
In your poem called 'Is'
I find catharsis.
I meant to quote a line
And say Thanks! How you've enriched mine!
But like a good poem it was a whole
It's Wyatt-like deceiving syncopocation only a role
To baffle the gullible pompous. They shy from raw soul.
The next thing, the new startler, seems too simple to be good,
Too close, impertinently personal. But they're polite, you're
     rude.
Like sex, babies, plants, animals and private life.
How alive, Kavanagh, how obstreperous you are in your grave,
Waiting, as you advised yourself,
Probably singing out of tune,
For time to pass, and what you did to be known.

Once you said I was all right
And I felt proud then,
But prouder now
When I read this poem and say Amen.

Parental Doubt

Doubt, parental doubt
Is a heavy sort of thing
To carry about.

Did you realise this
When you became pregnant,
My pretty miss?

That thirty years on
You might have a
Reproachful son,

Begun in love
But now saying 'Mother Mother
What were you thinking of?'

Do you realise, my dear,
Ecstatically knitting booties
That whatever you do you won't be able to please:
Your daughter says, 'Damn you, it's all your fault, my
    neurosis!

'You shouldn't have left me then
I'm all screwed up
I have to be mean to my man.'

Or even, 'You did too well!
Our childhood was one long paradise
Your glittering world turns out to be all lies:
Why didn't you give us a healthy taste of hell?'

Forty years on from there
When you see them puff and slip on the dangerous stair
Trying to get up and on
Will you be too old to care

If they now say, 'Mother Mother
We know what it's all about.
How did you cope with *your* parental doubt?'

What a bitch Dame Nature is,
My pretty miss,
Lucky you procreate in ignorant bliss.

The Useful Dead

Are alive people any more
Use than the dead are?
Is it better to ring up Hetta
Than open Byron?
Better to make a date to meet for a drink
Than look at the letters of Swift?
The dead cost you no money, effort, tact,
And they can't answer back.
They can't listen. But then
Neither do the living.
Well, hardly ever.
The dead can inspire, fire, seem to sympathise,
And can't hide under their lies
Which lie open, probed by inquisitive scholars
Conscientiously earning American dollars
Or a footnote in history. The marriage is rather blank
In bed with the dead. Is it better than a wank?
Is it fruitful or just instructive to flirt with Proust?
As a real-life friend he must have been one of the worst.
Don't telephone anyone: write it all down.
Maybe someone will understand you better after
  you're gone.

Winter Landscape

In the garden rotted bodies are fallen
Black leaves crashed
Asparagus pride decayed
Moss and creeping buttercup taking advantage
Of the mightier out-of-combat.

Still alive, birds hunched against hard times.
Burrowers, moles and mice and subterranean rats
Ravenous, ravage at the roots.

Mining

Little by little a little
But the gold lies low below
Even the best spade in an old hand
I know I know I know
Can't move the rubbish dump
If the faculties are limp.

The trustless tools are sharp
Well-tempered in the harp
But the tune lies low, buried and lost in the sand.
Keep faith. O faith I keep
But the bone can't feel the flesh.
There's an end to congress.

Year after year there falls
The leaves that time expels
Soil is spattered with sifting, silting, rotting.
I know these elementals
But where can the entrance be
To the mine in me?

Little by little a little
But the reckless miner digs
Minerals maddeningly there but perhaps not there.
O for the truffle dogs
To help divine where the helpless treasure's certain
And the last strength put out
On the right route.

Hangover

Diabolical Dionysius
Last night egged us on
To raze the sacred temples.
The god has gone.
Now troupes of mini-builders
Using their mini road drills
With puritanical fury
And vindictive zeal
Riot round *my* temples
Needed for enduring
This frail day.

Rhyme Is Wrong

Rhyme is wrong
For my irregular heart
It brings in ghostly masters
And sets the mind at puzzles
That's anyhow prone to baulk.
Am I burning the midnight oil
The candle at both ends
Sitting alone and hammering at my sores?
Shall I shut out the night
Faint vertical ash-tree lines?
For somebody watches from the top of the bank,
Never a friend, always inimical,
Why not a guardian angel on the job?
Then it would be all right
Not to shut out the night
And have to be far too closely cocooned with hammer
     and sores,
Trying out rhyme
Like a bandaid on a wound
That needs a surgeon and operating table
To do the least good.
For anyhow rhyme is wrong
For me and my lopsided song
And ghostly masters jeer
And the mind comes all over queer
And won't respond.

Margery Kempe

They fled from the boisterous sobbings of Margery Kempe
With fourteen children, husband and sins behind her
Now in her white and righteous robes
Noisily full of herself and her new vision
That plunged like a thunderbolt into her unread mind
And set her middle-aged legs
On the road to the Holy Land.
She couldn't write, so she had to make a noise.
They complained and avoided her company
(Especially in church
Where she really was outrageous
In the loud expression
Of her new-found passion).
An excessive lady
She tells us herself –
Far too fond of love
Even if the lover was her husband
And he, poor fellow,
Driven to incontinence and premature senility
(Another good reason for changing her direction).
A lovely terrible person
But a bit too much on a long dusty pilgrimage –
Better to travel with her now
When many centuries tone down the din.
A quiet Dutch scholar wrote it all down for her,
Bullied, no doubt, but his careful script never wavered,
And he kept his smiles suppressed
Till the self-revealing tale was told.

Are Flowers Whores?

Flowers aren't choosy
Which bee which bug
Come one come all.

Bees and bugs
Aren't choosy either
All entries sweetly natural.

Imagine a flower
Closing its throat
Against a bee it thought a bore.

Who said object
Should excite act
That *that* was moral?

If only the verb
The act acts,
Why call your sister a whore?

Sin and shame!
Abandon the word
Moral. You can *see* it's immoral.

NATURE NOTES

The Great Blue Spruce

The great blue spruce
has trouble carrying her babies:
The branches break
in the gusty spring gales
and the toasted tip clusters
nestled in the needles
lie in the dusty road –
a fabulous thrown-away work of art.

The Male Fruit

The male fruit
of the red pine
is not at all
like the round bouncy female:
but small and limp and curled
like a discouraged worm
it lies on the boards of my grey table
abandoned from above
with a few spent needles.

The Anxious Mother Spider

The anxious mother spider
with a giant ball of babies
staggers in a spidery way
across a desert of brown chips.
Elsewhere it is a brilliant summer's day
and the blue jays
seem to have no serious troubles.

A Little Newt

A little newt,
translucent orange,
still, and falsely safe
in the newly-turned sandy orange road,
exquisitely erroneous,
obeys his ancient genes.

I moved his vulnerable body
into the green jungle on the side.
He's saved, for the moment,
though perhaps at the cost of
considerable confusion of mind.

An Arrogant Snail

An arrogant snail
for purposes of his own
thought fit to cross
the gravelled road
at his own majestic pace.
And even if the cars flashed past
with a speed and fury
far beyond birds of prey,
so that he wouldn't even have time
to withdraw into his frail
shell,
still,
because they were so fast,
and he so slow,
he might have been missed,
and his unwise policy
justified.

Beaver

Beaver,
I liked that tail-slapping
on the waters of the
tangled pond.
It didn't seem serious,
more like an effete keeping up
of forms;
a salute to old wisdom,
now a bit of a bore,
but done perfunctorily,
just in case.

Two Dogs

I met two dogs in the wood.
We all stopped dead,
shocked by the unexpected.
Wolves? I thought,
distractedly trying to remember
where I was.
Humans? they thought in panic,
rigid with guilt
and their secret purpose
to lay a forbidden deer.
We went our separate ways,
shaken,
without a single sound.

Ladies' Tresses

Ladies' Tresses
is a lady-like white orchid,
found in New England
in damp sunny meadows,
inconspicuous
and self-effacing, but
immaculately righteous and upright
among the coarser weeds.

The Shepherd's Purse

How does the shepherd's purse,
newly germinated,
harried by geneological messages
urging him on
since the ice age,
suddenly feel
an unfriendly hand near,
dealing death
to all his tall relations,
and decide to change
into a perfect miniature,
so that a quick inconspicuous
propagation can take place?

Blake's Sunflower

1

Why did Blake say
'Sunflower weary of time?'
Every time I see them
they seem to say
Now! with a crash
of cymbals!
Very pleased
and positive
and absolutely delighting
in their own round brightness.

2

Sorry, Blake!
Now I see what you mean.
Storms and frost have battered
their bright delight
and though they are still upright
nothing could say dejection
more than their weary
disillusioned
hanging heads.